About the Author

Gamel Adulce' Abdullah, author of *Melting Pot of Sins: A Family Divided*, *The Hereafter*, *Led Astray* and *Read or Recite the Tree of Life*, now delivers his second book of poetry in *The Tree of Knowledge*. His new poetry is compiled with inspirational poetic verses that he has continued to write during his life experience, a journey that has brought forth wisdom by the grace and mercy of Allah. Gamel Abdullah has also published poetry with the International Library of Poetry and Noble House Publishers UK division. His poetry is included in seven anthologies between these two publishers. The International Library of Poetry selected Gamel Abdullah as a poetry ambassador for National Poetry

Month and Gamel Abdullah also received their Editor's Choice Award in 2006.

Gamel Abdullah was born on September 24, 1960 in the heart of North Philadelphia, better known as North Philly to native Philadelphians. He grew up one block from the famous Robin Hood Dell East in Fairmount Park. He was born to an African American Muslim couple, the late Nassardin and Sayeeda Abdullah. Gamel Abdullah relocated to New York City in 1994 but returned to his home town in 2000 and still resides in Philly to date.

Peace Until…

DISCLAIMER

The opinions and interpretations of religious books and texts expressed within this book are solely the author's and not those of the publisher.

Autobiography

We all are Authors and never touch a pen.
Two Scribes assigned, one for every deed of sin,
the other for righteousness within.
Two books will tell our stories, one of shame
the other of glory and pleasing The Publisher's
standards Foretold.
Many of our books will bomb fires burn and our souls
will be crushed for the sins we earned.
The scribe that documents with a righteous stroke
may save your book from fire and smoke!
The Publisher may call a sudden end to your story.
May your pages of sin weigh less than your righteous
glory?
May The Publisher award you His highest Honor
of Eternal Life in gardens of wonder…

Our Angels observing and documenting,
Our Creator knows the Autobiography of us all…
Peace Until…

THE TREE OF KNOWLEDGE

GAMEL ADULCE' ABDULLAH

THE TREE OF KNOWLEDGE

Vanguard Press

VANGUARD PAPERBACK

© Copyright 2022
Gamel Abdullah

The right of Gamel Abdullah to be identified as author of this work has been asserted by him in accordance with the Copyright, Designs and Patents Act 1988.

All Rights Reserved

No reproduction, copy or transmission of this publication may be made without written permission.
No paragraph of this publication may be reproduced, copied or transmitted save with the written permission of the publisher, or in accordance with the provisions of the Copyright Act 1956 (as amended).

Any person who commits any unauthorised act in relation to this publication may be liable to criminal prosecution and civil claims for damages.

A CIP catalogue record for this title is available from the British Library.

ISBN 978 1 80016 302 7

*Vanguard Press is an imprint of
Pegasus Elliot MacKenzie Publishers Ltd.*
www.pegasuspublishers.com

First Published in 2022

**Vanguard Press
Sheraton House Castle Park
Cambridge England**

Printed & Bound in Great Britain

Contents

Introduction 15
The Author is God 17
Chapter 1 Read or Recite the Tree of Life 19
Allah's Knowledge is Power Everlasting 21
Praising God 22
The Beauty of It All 23
Born 24
Signs Of Time 25
Past and Present 26
Defining Love 27
A Mother's Love 28
A Father's Love 29
Thinking of Mom 30
Thinking of Dad 31
Visions Of You 32
The Greatest Love Poem Ever Written 33
My Beloved 34
Moments Of Passion 35
Forgotten Love 36
Emotional Bliss 37
My Rising Sun 38
The Pleasure and Pain of Love 40
Smile My Son 41
Men Don't Cry 42

One Lie Told	43
Riverbanks Overflow	44
My Brother	45
Hearts Of Stone	47
Fabric And Land	48
Anticipation is a Sin	49
Casualties of War	50
Darkened Moral Days of Sin	51
Did We Forget?	52
The Tree of Life	53
The Author is God	54
Chapter 2 The Tree of Knowledge	55
The Tree of Knowledge	57
Beneath the Physical	58
Waiting in Tomorrow	59
Fast Forward	61
A Lowly Sinner's Thoughts	63
My Wife, My Love	64
Lead Yourself	65
We Never Die	66
Heaven: No Place for Racism	68
The Chief Judge	69
Love	70
Lost Love	71
Remember The Titans	72
Fight the Oppressor	74
The Messenger	75

To Exist, Thank Him Daily	76
The "I" Is the Most High	77
Led Astray by Tall Tail Lies	78
Face Your Fears	79
Eat Ye the Words of Truth	80
Levitation	82
Praise & Gratitude	83
The Comforting Departure	84
The Coming of the Hour	85
The Fix Is In	86
Stay Focused	87
Things Over Souls	89
North Philly Chapter 1	90
Message From the Author:	92
The Truth Hurts	92
The Comforter	95
God Hates Oppressors!	97
The Final Warning!	98
Once Clear Now Murky	100
Like A Woman	101
Not Even a Cure	103
The Soul	104

Introduction

To Allah be the praise and to Allah be the glory for He gave the gift to allow this story, the gift of the pen and words from within His powerful being that gives us the ability to read, recite and understand.

This life no accident no indeed, accidents don't produce words like these. Oceans twice deep, rivers twice wide if together were ink times five would not be enough to complete Allah's words that existed before our time. Before the creation of Heaven and Earth the word of Allah existed and brought forth manifested life. Allah simply said, "Be" and Life began.

The Author is God

Ocean twice deep
River twice wide
If they were Ink
Doubled times five
Not enough to complete
Words of infinity unique
Maya and Emily two of many
Fame benefits from infinity
Ocean twice deep
River twice wide
If they were Ink
Doubled times five
The greatest poets alive
Past and future twice deep
Twice wide doubled times five
Not enough to compete
His words will never die
Best Poet alive
Stated one word
"Be" and it was
Poetry lives on
The Author is God

I have compiled inspirational poetry that has entered my being over time in this life experience, a journey that has brought forth wisdom by the grace and mercy of our Creator who should be praised forever. I have included poetic verses from my first book of poetry titled, *Read or Recite the Tree of Life*.

I pray that you enjoy and are inspired by the poetic wisdom that heals my being and warns thy soul as you read, *The Tree of Knowledge*.

Chapter 1

Read or Recite the Tree of Life

Allah's Knowledge is Power Everlasting

Created pure not tainted or stained
Upheld above all Allah shaped and molded man
In a state of happiness he so wanted him to be
Gave him choice and set him free
Gardens of roses far as the eye could see
Suddenly whispers from some boldly proud being
Created pure not tainted or stained
Polluted by a whisper of treachery and hate
Unseen deception by one moved far from the gate
Forgot to follow the Master's plan
Lost now is the state of man
Created pure not tainted or stained
Rain water, food by the grace of His hand
Knowledge of His wisdom lays across the land
Pathways back to His promise gate
Gardens of everlasting peace await
Mankind following lies of treachery and hate
Whispers repeated by progeny of the unseen snake
Hell grows hungry as we choose our fate
Gardens of bliss await smiles of eternal greetings of peace
One brotherhood, one family in complete happiness
The righteous will be pure not tainted or stained
One with Allah is the plan for man
Knowledge is power wisdom is gained

Praising God

Nothingness to Something less
Darkness falls as lights progress
Water filled development grows
Brown to greens all colors now show
Land water star filled sky
Sun moon clouds pass by
Creatures moving alive and cloned
Humanity born from mud and rib bone
Seven days does a week make?
Twelve months does a year calculate?
All this; have you ever wondered why
Why He made nothing to something for you and I.
You ever show gratitude thank Him each day
For Nothingness could return as we fade away
Thanking and Praising God each time I Pray
Do you take for granted the sun will rise?
May darkness fall upon ungrateful eyes?
Praising God

The Beauty of It All

Silence till first sounds of winged creatures singing
Darkness till first light peeks on sun lit horizons
Slow winds bring to life colors of all brands
Flowers and trees spread across beautiful lands
Water sparkle reflections as sunbeams show
Sustenance plentiful in waters deep or dry land grow
Delightful flavors from grape vines sweet fed by hand
Horizon dims, stars begin as the moon races the sun
Creatures, all kinds now rest so to rise and stand tall
Oh my Lord, the Beauty of it All.

Born

Light shines strange and bright
Moving touching feelings of slow flights
Changing so strange from dark days past
Suddenly feeling sharp pain on bare hind
Screaming and breathing for the very first time
Peaceful and graceful were dark days before
Avenue of sustenance cut and now sore
The feeling of hunger goes as lips strain
Returning back to dark days past
Slowly, slowly remembering with gasp
Suddenly, suddenly awaken with haste
Who delivered me to this horrible place?
Visions of crimes and Humanity hate
Oh, Allah, please open your gates
Return Thy Soul from this strange place

Signs Of Time

Trust now lost
Eyes blind shut
Souls need help
Pain felt hearts
End time signs
Joyful immoral minds
Sorrowed moral hearts
Earth now dark
End now near
Souls tremble with fear
Father kills son a sin
Son kills Father and grins
Brother kills Brother
Man marries Man
Women marries Women
Sunup no light
Mountains not in sight
Full moon blood shot red
Mankind now dead
Quiet Earth stands
All rolled up in the Creator's Hand
Judgment awaits the sinful Man

Past and Present

Elders fading fast prolonged life in an hourglass
How great the days long traveled roads passed
All summed up with a final breath gasped
Much good forgotten powerful knowledge lost
Remember the days before polluted air by street cars
Cobblestone streets Fruit Man calling afar
Get your fresh fish silver trout I got watermelon he would shout
Front door open all night till dawn no need for alarms
Children respected elders and played stick ball
Double Dutch hide and seek with sounds of pitter-patter from
their young innocent feet
Grandpop Grandmom no strangers then
Elders wise and counseled their Kin
Now those in present dark days of sin
Lock your doors keep children safe within
The Beast flies with lies from Devil's cry in Him
Wisdom fades past, dark souls lost in an hourglass

Defining Love

What is Love many have asked?
To Define at times words fade past
A challenge for many so hard the task
The task of understanding Love you ask
What is Love and why at times pain
The answer you seek is buried within
Within the stone heart beneath the skin
How to retrieve an answer from stone
Walk with me as I guide you home
I'll tell you a story to find your way
The way for you to turn stone to clay
What do you mean by this turning trick?
Oh my Beloved of surety no trick
Hold my hand as I cure the sick
Walk with me as I clothe the poor
Feed them feed them give them more
My oh my how they turn and cry
They truly adore you as you pass by
When you care for those in need
Love is born from your stone like seed.

A Mother's Love

One with you my life began. One with you and our Love grew to be one Love shared between two. A Mother's Love, who can compare, with the Love a Mother has to share with many or just a few? Never ending Love continuous and true Oh how I long for you when I'm unsure of what to do. A Mother's Love, who can compare? With pleasure and pain she produced you and me, with Love and devotion she raised us to be righteous Beings as God oversees. A Mother's Love, who can compare? As I lose my way in life as I fail in fighting off my fears I cry out for my Mother so dear, where is my Mother I long for her ever Loving beautiful smile and embrace as only she can secure on her God sent face. Honor thy parents for God does state and Honor the womb that bore you God reiterates. Peace be with her for she gives up much in this life, for her child she does sacrifice. A Mother's Love who can compare?

A Father's Love

A Father's Love is at times shadowed by the Ever presence of A Loving Mother's embrace but his Love is no less. A Loving Father will not be blessed to spend all of his day with his child, work must be done to shelter, feed and clothe his son. At times he is sorrowed because he can't seem to attain his dream, his dream of giving his son the best of things. He must have patience during difficult times, continue to pursue, Allah will provide until in time he can do. Sometimes it seems his dreams just won't come true, all he can do is continue to pursue. What a Father does for his child at times can't be seen, unlike the Loving Mother who is always there to embrace, a Loving Father must always keep the faith and pray that someday his child will understand. A Loving Father, who can compare, A Loving Father will always be there. Save the Children.

Thinking of Mom

Deep within dark channel free from light
Pleasurable minds from bodies of might
Passionate Love between Beings sweet
Planted seeds lie between thighs deep
You carry me now no sign of your feet
Wondering if his love is the same
Months pass by discomfort and pain
Contemplating what shall be thy name
Long awaited days anticipating change
Suddenly, suddenly while pushing with strain
My how you wonder at God's gift to Man
You hold me feed me protecting with care
I look up and feel you'll always be there
Mother, my Mother, you nourished with Love
Thanking Him daily God up above
If not for Mothers Humanity may die
Thinking of Mom on this Mother's Day cry.

Thinking of Dad

You think you're fast? A question asked of a Son from his Dad. I'll race you to the corner and give you a head start. OK, take your mark. From the word go running fast for a short while the little Boy never saw the joy from his Dad's smile. He ran thinking of only winning as he stretched for the finish line, a young Boy thinking of being a track star all the time. The thought never crossed His mind that he would lose to his Dad. He heard the strong sounds of his Dad's footsteps as he passed, His dreams faded fast. Nothing could compare that day with the race I shared with my Dad. Oh! How I loved to see the joy on his face from just a short race between a Son and his Dad.

Visions Of You

As I lay but not asleep
All night visions while eyes wide fixed
My mind fantasizing as I toss and turn
Creating endless endings of my own
Only yesterday did we meet
Since that moment not a day's sleep
Until tomorrow as I turn
My body gives in for the rest it yearns
I close my eyes but suddenly wake
I almost lost you to a day of sleep

The Greatest Love Poem Ever Written

Traveling long journeys, free of emotional Completeness. Concentrations of oneness not blended for perfection. Experiencing colorful Beings on many textured roads; Many exits taken until your beautiful unblemished soul. My eyes did capture your smile as if it were my own. Wanting you to call out to the thorny rose exposed. Shedding thorns to comfort your passionate embrace; My how the Lord created such a beautiful warm face. Visions of you mirrored in my mind to eyes fixed. Remembering the first time when our lips first kissed. Passions of silk and satin smooth like water flow. Never letting go, Never letting go, Never letting go. Traveling journey now emotionally complete; Found the true Love that I once set out to seek. My heart does bleed as my eyes do tear with fear, that one day you will no longer be here to share Our Passions of Silk and Satin in Fields of Roses without Thorns.

My Beloved

From the Depths of My Mind
From the Depths of My Soul
From the Deep Seas of My Heart
As it Bleeds These Words
I Love You
Until Souls Meet Twice
Hereafter Eternally
My Beloved Wife

Moments Of Passion

Moments of Passion seem everlasting
Waiting your return seems like forever
Seeing you from time to time is not enough
I long for your tender endless touch
Sun up to sun down all night till dawn
I tremble just before the moment we touch
Just one touch ignites the earth to move
Small tremors lead to volcanic eruptions
Flowing with emotions of exotic Passions
As I taste sweet flavors of your satin skin

Forgotten Love

Once the beacon that you traveled to find
The only light you kindled was mine
Now you trade me for diamonds and gold
No longer a part of your once beautiful soul
Still in your life but forgotten it seems
Material things now consume your dreams
My soul starves for your tender touch
Passion it craves embraces that clutch
Night after night I toss and turn
Fighting the sin that my mind does yearn
No longer in the eye of the beholder's dream
How long do I wait before cutting the seam
Sin does tempt me during times as I wait
Adultery Fornication my mind contemplates
Why oh why do you ignore me now
Full circle of love turned upside down
Bottle of emotions waiting to explode
Searching for another to share my soul
As the sun rises with your diamonds and gold
Lost me for greed and a heart turned cold

Emotional Bliss

A special day for emotional bliss
Visions of you awaiting your kiss
I dare not give you trinkets of gold
I dare not give you flowers or pearls
To explain or lie may stain your soul
So I give you my heart with patience and peace
As our love grows with this day of emotional bliss
Peace and Blessings

My Rising Sun

In a daze contemplating, evaluating, hesitating
My mind deep in thought while alone but yet not
Where am I to go, what am I to do? Was my plot
Visions of living beings passing but invisible am I
Invisible until a twinkle below my brow's brown eyes

Contemplating, evaluating, hesitating
Could it be the rising of the sun or the moon?
From a twinkle to a beacon healing my darkroom
Guiding me from the depths of my dark thoughts
Such a beautiful vision my brown eyes caught

Contemplating, evaluating, hesitating
All was still without motion for a moment in time
It was neither the sun nor moon that gazed my eyes
It was God's gift to man when He saw him sad
Radiant was your smile dark thought now lost
Hesitating due to heart twice tossed

Contemplating, should I speak a word or lust
Evaluating her hips and striding curves thrust
Hesitating with words flowing in my poetic mind
Do I want a broken heart for the third time?
Beautiful Black Woman competition is none

Your smile blinded me like the rising of the sun
With seductive island tones flowing from your tongue
 Contemplating, evaluating, hesitating now done.
 Desiring you; God's gift my beautiful rising sun.

The Pleasure and Pain of Love

Love is pleasure and pain
360 degrees of yin and yang
180 degrees of pleasure
As we walk hand in hand together
bodies tingling with anticipation
Hearts pounding emotions racing
Sweat pouring earth quaking
Sun rises darkness awakens
Anticipating 180 degrees of yin
Singing Love songs in spring
180 degrees of pain from yang
Singing the blues heart broken twice
180 degrees of hate no Love here tonight
Building bricks of emotional walls
No anticipation as darkness falls
Heart felt pain pleasure now lost
Pray our Love is stronger than pain
May yin bring forth balance to yang
May our Hearts sing spring songs again
As we travel the full circle of Love

Smile My Son

Smile now lost pain felt heart
Remembering joyful days lost
Embraces once close now apart
Emotional pain love tossed
Never meant to hurt or cross
Fixed strained blood stained eyes
Tears flow memories cause pain
Will we ever be Friends again?
Much lost in a life of Sin
Children crying anger shows
Relationship drowning; lies still flow
Never meant to hurt or cause pain
Eyes bloodshot red and stained
Will we ever be Friends again?
Reaching out to repair damage done
Ignore forgiveness heart never won
What I would give for a smile from my Son

Men Don't Cry

Who told the lie Men don't cry?
Years holding back war brewing inside
Cried like a baby when Dad died
Who told this bold lie?
Who told the lie Men don't embrace?
Makes them weak, soft and easy to break
Embraced my son just yesterday
Made me feel strong when he kissed my face
Beware of pride talk and lies foretold
Emptiness grows in hearts of stone
God created the emotions within
Tears and Love are not a sin.

One Lie Told

One lie told by a bitter scorned soul
Good Character crushed viewed with distrust
Once admired in all the land
Respect given from soft earth to dry sand
Envied by some, Loved by others
Expressions of hate this lie did create
A women scorned produced this fate
One lie told by a bitter scorned soul
Good Character crushed viewed with distrust
Believable tears and emotional lows
A women scorned by her own lies told
Lost her man angry and despised
Truth be told the love never died
Wanting to turn back the hands of time
Respect given like forced winds
Love given by family and friends
Praying the truth be told in the end

Riverbanks Overflow

The river flows and stands still from highs
and lows. Try to control a river raging
almost impossible to contain. Emotions rain
down feeding the river as it overflows.
Running down smooth mountainsides as it
separates. I try to contain the waters as my
emotions feed the swell. I attempt to absorb
the spillage as it is now a rage parallel.
Why do emotions feed the riverbanks so to
cause overflow? Emotional lows seem
to flow out of control. The river is always
in a rage when winds of anger show. Sometimes
when I smile the river begins to swell. I
attempt to control the emotional high and
wipe my river away. At times it's a joy to
watch the rivers running as smiles from faces glow.

My Brother

My Brother came like the silence of night
No Cross did he bear No Crescent in sight
No Star of David or books to recite
My Brother came like the silence of night

My Brother came like the silence of night
While you waited for symbols as signs
You missed the Messenger as He passed by
My Brother came like the silence of night

My Brother came like the silence of night
His character humble, kind and giving
His smile welcomed all of the living
My Brother came like the silence of night

My Brother came like the silence of night
He did not speak from the Bible book
He was the book with each step he took
My Brother came like the silence of night

My Brother came like the silence of night
To guts and ghettos where many dare flight
No church, mosque or synagogue for his work
His mission to save souls down in the dirt

God sends Messengers for many reasons
My Brother Dee Messenger for all seasons

Do you remember the love he gave?
Do you remember the time he forgave?
Do you remember when he fed and clothed?

Remember My Brother for the Love that He Showed

Duane, although our time was short, Our Love is Everlasting

Peace Until Souls Meet Twice. Your Brother Forever
Your Brother for Life With Love As I Write.

In Loving Memory of 'My Brother' Duane Francis
12/14/1996 to 4/21/2004

Hearts Of Stone

Hearts of stone
Cold barren so alone
Deceived raped beaten tricked
Prejudice racism butt kicked
Not realizing the stone is sick
Only 'One' can cure or fix
Beaming lights now transfixed
Pages turn feeding dark pits
Moral knowledge now consumed
God now welcomed in your dark room
Only He can soften the stone
As you submit He welcomes you home
Forgiveness is hard at times it seems
Except when you follow His way His dreams
Stone begins to soften like clay
Love is now on its way
Keep the Faith

Fabric And Land

Land and Fabric, Fabric and Land, so many have succumbed to this pride of Man. With Fabric in hand waved across the Land, each Man divided on which He stands. Fabric and Land so colorful the two, one made by Man the other, God credit is due. Land and Fabric so foolishly used, one we take pride in the other we abuse.

If the Fabric burns, could cost you a term, abuse the Land and there's no concern. Fabric and Land do we shed blood, bodies lie lifeless all for the pride of colorful cloth. Why no Fabric to clothe the poor, why no Land to shelter your eye sore? Fabric and Land our Brothers did die. Land and Fabric our Mothers still cry. Fabric and Land you wave for war your greed for Land you do fight for. When will you learn, Fabric has no concern for the breath of life we live on? Fabric and Land, Power and Greed, burn the damn Flag and get on Your knees, Pray God forgives your past deeds.

Anticipation is a Sin

Anticipation is a sin while loading your gun,
Noose, chain to cause pain
Anticipation is a sin can't wait to place
Your worldwide lie for all to see and force
The hand of those who don't agree
Anticipation is a sin waiting until night
Fall or sun rise to drop bombs again
Anticipation is a sin lying so to kill to
Steal black liquid gold to control
Anticipation is a sin waiting for the married
soul to enter your den again or planning to
take control of an innocent young soul
Anticipation is a sin wanting to tell the
Beggar no again as you grin

Anticipation is not a sin as we race the wind
anticipating victory for the opposite of
these sins within

Casualties of War

Casualties of war oh what an eyesore!
Babies dying bodies flying death at our doors
Collateral Damage used loosely today
As if leaving out fact the infants you attacked
Will deliver a soft blow to those without a clue
Children you killed with powerful skill
Mothers you burned as you use this term
Collateral Damage to cover your shame
As you murder grandparents walking with canes!
Couldn't be God fearing uttering these words
For these are words of Power and Greed
God counting their evil deeds as they proceed
Towards the day sacred Collateral will be damaged
Evil souls dying repeatedly
A just recompense for the Greedy
Oh! What an eye sore, true Casualties of War.
Keep the Faith!

Darkened Moral Days of Sin

Darkened moral days as unto night fall
Man and Jinn amused as shadows crawl
Faithless shameless lies within
Flesh and spirit together in sin
Bottomless pit welcomes them in
Punishment for those amusing grins

Faithful souls patiently waiting
The Lord our God, contemplating
No matter how dark the days have become
They cherish new blooms and the rising sun
They cherish waterfalls, oceans and streams
They cherish the stars and moon that beams
They cherish new life cut from the seam

Holding firm to cherished faith within
Forsaking the darkened moral days of sin

Did We Forget?

Did we forget the threat of the bottomless pit?
A blazing heat that torments without quit
Centuries have passed since witnessing His wrath
Immoral souls travel the heedless paths
Did we forget the Judgment Day?
When all in the graves will rise from clay
Those in sin will tremble with fear
They did forget their Lord was near
Did we forget His promise of Life?
Eternally granted to souls raised twice
Who righteously lived out their first journey?
And remembered to pray: 'To God be the Glory!'

The Tree of Life

Read or Recite the tree of life
Eat of this tree eternal bliss
Everlasting life of endless happiness
Rivers and streams of milk; honey and wine
Fields of petals, flowers of various kinds
Be warned of the tree of fruit and thorn
To eat of it evil is born
Eternally happy bare without stain
One bite, now covered with shame
Walking the Earth of pleasure and pain
Desiring again to read or recite
In the endless Garden of the tree of life
Keep the faith Heaven awaits!

The Author is God

Ocean twice deep
River twice wide
If they were Ink
Doubled times five
Not enough to complete
Words of infinity unique
Maya and Emily two of many
Fame benefits from infinity
Ocean twice deep
River twice wide
If they were Ink
Doubled times five
The greatest poets alive
Past and future twice deep
Twice wide doubled times five
Not enough to compete
His words will never die
Best Poet alive
Stated one word
"Be" and it was
Poetry lives on
The Author is God

Chapter 2

The Tree of Knowledge

"Knowledge Is Power Wisdom Is Gained."

The Tree of Knowledge

The Tree of Knowledge has fully bloomed.
What was forbidden has been consumed.
Good and Evil now fills your dark room.
Your eternal fate depends on a simplistic choice
So choose wisely and take heed of the guiding voice.
What was forbidden has been consumed.
Right versus Wrong now fill your dark room.
Lost your way to the Paradise Gate
Make no mistake, voice of the snake leads far from Good fate,
The Gate to the Garden where Paradise awaits…
And it will be said, Now eat of the Tree of Life Eternal
And Forever Enjoy the Mercy of Your Lord…

Beneath the Physical

From head to toe beautiful,
Successfully mastering the physical,
Compliments daily,
Ignored rarely,
Heads turn, lust and moans,
Yes, the physical wets their lips,
You're more than thighs and hips,
Yes, it's the first attraction,
We give each other satisfaction,
Not only physical but emotional attachments,
Loving you daily,
Ignoring you rarely,
Beneath the physical they can't see,
Your heart is only meant for me…

Poetry for my wife, Shanta

Waiting in Tomorrow

I'm waiting in tomorrow, seems like tomorrow will never come, all it takes is one less breath and we'll be as in the flesh but our spirits thrive in tomorrow.

Be true, be good, no rush I am waiting. Live life naturally, no debating. One less breath is all it takes, it will come naturally, you are in yesterday I'm free.

I'm waiting in tomorrow, seems like tomorrow will never come, all it takes is one less breath and we'll be as in the flesh but our spirits thrive in tomorrow.

I see you as you sleep waiting the appearance in your dreams, missing you too, only your heart and my soul know the means.

You live in yesterday and I'm waiting in tomorrow, seems like tomorrow will never come, all it takes is one less breath and we'll be as in the flesh but our spirits thrive in tomorrow.

You think tomorrow will never come, it will come like in your dreams, we are meant to last forever. Be true, be good live life naturally. One less breath is all it takes, yesterday our memories, we thrive in tomorrow.

I'm waiting in tomorrow, seems like tomorrow will never come, all it takes is one less breath and we'll be as in the flesh but our spirits thrive in tomorrow.

Tomorrow we will be as one, united forever, the promise of the Most High.

Fast Forward

Fast Forward to a better place
Fast Forward from this forsaken place.

Wish he never took a taste now we
Know good and evil within us, the
Leaves never covered our shame enough.
"Get ye down from thus,"
Went from fully covered to a string up her butt,
now a place where fame overshadows shame.

Knowing that we must complete this trial,
A choice we have of good or badness,
wrong choice eternal sadness.

Fast Forward to this sacred place
Where the first man created relaxed
in peace while loving his mate.

Just a taste from a forbidden source,
just a whisper from an Evil force and this
tranquil place now out of reach until the right
choice is made before a seeming eternal sleep.

This place of choice continuously
Revolving, volatile but yet beautiful

Earth. This Earth has become a
More problematic quake due to the
Evil choices Mankind can't seem to shake.

So Fast Forward to this place of
Tranquility, this place of complete
Happiness and never ending love for Humanity.

Oh God! Patience we must endure,
For sure this tranquil place is prepared
For us but we may not be prepared
for this glorious door.

Desires not to wait, Fast Forward
Because we hate the taste of this
Present place called Earth.

Transformation of the Earth to
Paradise for those who are Righteous
to inherit as we earn and merit our future home…

Allah Knows Best who we are,
Praying for forgiveness for us all…

A Lowly Sinner's Thoughts

From the words of a lowly sinner wisdom is taught.
From the breath of life given, life is worth living with eternal happiness being the end goal.
An earthly trial set, perfection never met requesting forgiveness your safety net.
Message clear with faith and fear the Unseen judges with all fairness. One God worship with cleanliness, righteousness the lesson, love the blessing and the sum of it all.
Opposition the life of the sinner still forgiven before this physical life trial ends. All learned in this life of sin, scrolls past down time and time again, not complicated as wisdom sinks in.
The Hereafter our goal, eternal life unfolds with happiness foretold as we measure our faith in thought. To know a good tree by the fruit that it bears you first have to learn the tree, please forgive me for this charitable thought for I'm just a lowly sinner taught.
Acknowledge and Praise Him daily…

My Wife, My Love

My Wife, my Love
At first sight I knew.
Compliment was given minutes few.
Your beauty magnetic.
Thoughts of your perfection
Not yet a word spoken
Intimidating, no preparation
Competition upon you daily
Not bold enough to cut in line
Waiting for just the right time
Years drifting by you on my mind
Suddenly a twinkling in my eye
The future was shown at first sight
The time was finally right
Not at all easy
Getting to know you became pleasing
My African Queen, A beauty rarely seen
So amazing as a moonlit night
So amazing and now my beautiful Wife!
My Love…

Lead Yourself

I'm a Leader but don't follow me!
I may fail during this life's calamity.
No excuse not to attain your destiny.
It's never too late to learn to read.
It's never too late to learn to lead.
It's never too late to plan to succeed.
The Creator taught the use of the pen.
Our memories may fail us within.
Read and recite the lessons daily.
Ask questions for clarity,
from one whose wisdom is noted.
History: Many failed followed lambs.
Led astray by fellow man.
Lead Yourself to the Promised Land!
Knowledge is Power
Wisdom is gained.

We Never Die

The Creator: "Say not of those who pass that they are dead, they are not dead, their souls return to from which they first came."

No one dies a permanent death, only the wise will understand my spoken breath…

No, not tangible for most but faith in the promise of the Unseen keeps our eyes on the prize…

The pure light spirits gently remove the souls of the righteous at the time of their passing. They will view the earthly sorrows of their loved ones as their shell remains until dust proclaims…

The pure light spirits violently rip the souls of the non-believers at the time of their passing. They too will view the earthly sorrows of their loved ones as their shell remains until dust proclaims.

The state of our everlasting existence is our choice: For the righteous, a life of eternal happiness without want or need.

For the non-believers an eternal life in the burning Hell Fires!

There will be sorted groups and we will all see or be with our loved ones.

The question is, in what group will your final destination be?

Example of your Resurrection Day:

Green to Brown grass upon the ground as seasons turn around so will Mankind…
If you are reading this now you still have a chance to change, how will you choose?

Heaven: No Place for Racism

The Creator's Message to Mankind:
And among His signs are the creation of the Heavens and the Earth, and the diversity of your languages and colors. Surely in this are signs indeed for people who have knowledge (of the facts in creation, and who are free of prejudices).
O mankind! We created you from a single (pair) of a male and a female, and made you into nations and tribes, that ye may know each other not that ye may despise (each other). Verily the most honored of you in the sight of Allah is (he who is) the most righteous of you. And Allah has full knowledge and is well acquainted (with all things).
I have given you your Colors and languages not to despise each other but to know each other.
*We live in a racist society so I'm not surprised that we get sidetracked so often. 'The great divide, the great self-pride in color, land or flag.' Racism so deep seated that we stand by and protect the evil deeds of our race and fail to measure their deeds based on righteousness.
Our true family in the Hereafter will be those amongst you who are Righteous to be inclusive of all nations, colors and genders…

The Chief Judge

You may rejoice over man's laws approved in your favor, allowing you to wallow in sins of immoral dangers. Be pleased with yourself but for a temporary time, the Chief Judge has made up His Masterful mind. Respite granted in this life of sin. Forgiveness offered with rope extend, hopefully guided away from the folly within. Time is ticking with an unknown end.
A Messenger told not to despair at the hate displayed for I am near. I created the law it is Me they hate! Very soon I will proclaim their fate!
No appeals will be granted when the Chief Judge calls the end of this Earthly trial. His Judgement Day awaits as the Righteous smiles.
Oh! How you stray far from His Books, His Laws disregarded, His Grace overlooked.
Splendor now Oh ye hear! Splendor now, soon your soul will shake with fear!

Love

Love, an emotion that has always existed before the creation of all things within and beyond the universe. Love exists in all beings, for those who have found this emotion within can't contain the tears that naturally overflow when witnessing signs of joy, sorrow, pain, kindness for those in need and know that this emotion is the key to eternal happiness.

Love is absorbed by the soft heart much sooner than the hard heart. The hard heart repels the emotion of love due to a lack of acceptance of true knowledge and accepting prideful tales that showing love is a sign of weakness.

Oh Mankind, Oh my Brothers and Sisters, my parents, my sons and daughters, Oh my family, my friends, my neighbors! Love is the key to eternal happiness and its signs are caring, kindness, giving to those in need, praying for those who are ill or in want.

The signs of Love are declining as we thrive on hateful intentionally produced drama filled media.

A reminder for all Mankind, "You know a good tree by the fruit that it bears!" Let us all begin planting trees that bear good fruit!

An Eternal Life of Happiness will be the reward for those who are Righteous and learn to Love one another so sayeth the Lord our God and Creator of all things!

Lost Love

Sorrowful heart
Sorrowful mind
Knot in the throat
Pain down the spine.
Lost someone close, the first time.
Pain felt heart
Pain felt mind
How long will this last
This painful prison of mine.
Some grieve for a day
Others a lifetime
For this moment I miss you
Lost love of mine.
You're in every dream
Reaching for you as I wake
You're not here what a heart break
Loving you in memory
The pain really ending me
Accepting that you're gone
Eating at the best of me
Happiness we shared
Praying the Hereafter is near
Will we really be one again?
Oh! How I pray for this with faith not fear.
For All Who Struggle with Passing Loved Ones.

Remember The Titans

I remember the Titans
When my Good Brother stood up
Stood up to racism, Oh how corrupt
Woodbury NJ the seen
A white man's problem
A black man's dream
We walked in together
a restaurant theme.
The good old boys smiling
plotting to end good things.
I see you're walking your monkey
One good old boy screamed.
My Good Brother Mike Stood up
Not to fight but to state what was right.
Watch the company you keep he
Stated to the good old boy that night.
In the land of the Klan he stood up.
Stood up for a fellow man against those who were corrupt!
A white man Stood up for a black man in the land of the Klan…
I was a leader, he was my right hand man.
We made things possible
together working hand in hand.

In a land where equality no matter the race, religion, color or creed is well quoted but still a good dream.
I feel this day it's a reality between good friends.
Thinking of my friend, Good Brother
Michael Lanigan.
Racism is not natural, it is taught! Our young children show us this fact before they enter school while at the playground playing catch, chasing a ball or brushing away a friend's tears after a brief fall…
If we can enjoy each other's company during a sports event, it is very possible to enjoy each other in everyday life events. Hint hint!
Today I measure Human Beings on the Good or Evil they produce not by their race, religion, color or creed.
God forgives, just ask Him…
Remembering the Titans!

Fight the Oppressor

I once was a G man carried a rifle with pack in hand. Shipped me off to some foreign land, learned I may be killing my Brother man. Oh! This was not in my goals or plan. Now confused headed for Sun baked sands.
They proved no respect for my religion or me as a man. I decided my separation plans. Yes, me the former G man.
No honor for the flag or the land for which it stands if it leads towards corruption to kill my brother man.
Who was the enemy? Where do I point my gun? Both sides prayed toward the east of the rising Sun.
God gives us choice as a part of His plan to live free of oppression or tyranny in His land.
If this exists you have the right to leave or fight by any means necessary until the oppressors take flight…
Do you know your Enemy?

The Messenger

From the Creator's Mouth
To the Angel's ear
A message delivered swiftly
Delivered without fear
An unlettered Prophet
The message did reach
A Prophet not rehearsed to preach
Never once taught to read or write
The Angel Gabriel inspired
The Prophet to recite.
So the Chosen One spoke words
From time to time
As the Angel delivered inspiration
When commanded by God
Today known as the Holy Qur'an!
114 Chapters, 286 verses from an illiterate man?
You missed the Miracle! All He Has To Say Is "Be"
And It Is…
Seek and ye shall find,
Knowledge is Power,
Wisdom is gained.

To Exist, Thank Him Daily

Let There Be Light Called, Lasting Darkness Falls…
Universe Created, A Special Place Designated…
All He Planned And Designed, No Accidental Kind…
Many Creatures Created, Oh! What A Masterful Mind…
Special Plan Set Aside For Those To Be Called Mankind!
What A Beautiful Feeling To Know You Exist!
Every Thoughtful Memory Of Love And Of Bliss…
Pondering Thoughts Of Nothingness, Oh My! How I Hate This.
Thanking Him Each Day For Eternal Existence!
Know Thy Self, Love Thy Self…

The "I" Is the Most High

For Example: If I thought of creating something out of nothing…
I named that something, "You".
I gave You speech…
I gave You hearing…
I gave You vision…
I gave You the breath of life…
I gave You sustenance…
I gave You shelter…
I gave You knowledge and understanding…
I gave You a Wife and the ability to replicate everything that I have given You, now through Her mixed with pleasure and Love while doing so…
And Once You see the beautifully replicated new Life, You give all praise to Your Wife…
After All "I" have given You, how in the sake of continued existence do You fail to give "I" Your praise and Your gratitude!
"Thou shalt not bow down thyself to them, nor serve them: for I the LORD thy God am a jealous God,"
Take Note, Last Quote A Bible Quote…
Trinity? Or One God!

Led Astray by Tall Tail Lies

I wish there was an indicator when you faked Y2K…
Fools spent much money that day…
You also lied about the Rapture, 244 souls only to be saved riding off to heaven in a spacecraft while the rest of us burn…
Your prophecies of religious Judgment Day dates have come and gone,
how did you get that one wrong? Aztec Calendar also now frowned upon…
I knew I should have stood firm with the Holy Qur'an!
Don't Be Fooled! There is an Indicator!

Face Your Fears

I found My Self beneath a flat rock in the sea holding on tight with barely enough air to breathe afraid the sea may drown me…
I found My Self on top of a flat rock surrounded by miles of sea holding on tight for fear the sea may drown me…
I found My Self kicking and pulling the water daring not to stop in fear the sea may drown me…
I found My Self holding tightly the trunk of a tree in fear that hurricane force winds would blow me back to sea and drown me…
I found My Self walking on dry land pondering I was safe and slipped into a hole of quicksand and the land drowned me…
No matter what we do we will never avoid the first passing so face your fears head on, enjoy life until it drowns you.
The Resurrection brings forth a brighter day for those who Believe!

Eat Ye the Words of Truth

From the Bringer of Truth, One Who is endued with wisdom and knowledge!
The Angel Jibril (Gabriel) delivered the Holy Qur'an from the Highest Spiritual College!
It states: Isa (Jesus) will be a sign of the coming of the hour!
Isa and Maryam (Mary) will be honored in this world and in the Hereafter!
White woolly hair, Bronze skin and eyes like a flame of fire! He will be found among those who bend at the knee and showered with honor!
It's a shame, by this descriptor's signs of what would be met by discrimination this day, Isa (Jesus) would be shot as a minority invader or a terrorist of our Nation's prejudicial ways!
Evangelist and false Prophets lied to You!
Failed Rapture Dates passed as you waited in pew!
Nostradamus scientifically and historically wrong!
Big Bang Accidental, Evolution or just another Spiritual pollution?
Mayans' Calendar Wrong, date passed, long gone as you wait in spiritual song.
The Holy Qur'an: "No One Knows The Coming Of The Hour!" The answer is with Allah alone.

So, my brothers and Sisters don't be a lamb, be a leader! Study to show yourself approved and stop the false Prophets, Preachers, Priests, Pastors, Rabbis and Imams when they invent new lies and repeat old lies. Defeat them in powerful and truthful argument!
Food for thought…

Levitation

Levitating in my dreams,
Body in flight no powerful wings,
A spiritual connection so it seems,
Slowly gliding beneath the clouds,
Inspirational Angel shows me how,
Journey taken far and wide,
Feeling special a spiritual pride,
Adoring creation His power and grace,
Awaiting the day I see His face,
When I awake, this dream so real,
Anticipating another spiritual flight,
When absent, I question, am I living right?
Back to the Book, continued prayers, falling asleep as my Angel prepares…
Eternal Life, Prepare Your Flight!

Praise & Gratitude

There will not be one person left on this Earth that will not experience separation from its self of itself.
One part will remain, returned to the Earth from which it came. The other ascends back to the Creator who is known by many Names!
By design no accident, show your gratitude and praise to the One and Only God! Yes, be amazed!
By His Glory and His Wrath the Believers follow His path.
We shall live forever, no one really dies… It will be the state of Eternal Happiness or Eternal Hell Fire no compromise!
Oh! He is the Most Gracious, the Most Merciful and The Often Forgiving, just a few of His many Names.
Seeking His Face and Pleasure should be your real aim to fame, for in the Hereafter His Pleasure is far better than Eternal pain…
Praise Him Daily, Show Your Gratitude! How will you choose?

The Comforting Departure

I closed my eyes but not asleep
Not yet dreaming as the stardust peaked.
Golden sparkling stardust starting a graceful swirl, a bright like star near the top as it turned gracefully within darkness.
Glittering swirling side to side but upward bound, floating in space a uniformed stardust without sound.

The star seemed to give it light and life as it gracefully moved round as if it were dancing before a silent glittering night.
And then I saw her without a frown, her beautiful smile, her youthful glow, her dimples, her high cheek bones, her long Indian heritage nose and her hair laid back like feathers in rows, her beautiful face floating within and out of the golden glittering stardust as it gracefully moved about.
I could feel the tears well up pass the lashes and down my cheekbones, as I smiled with my mom knowing she was finally free.
Her trial was over as emotions overwhelmed me.
Her Creator did command the Angels to gently guide her soul back to the Throne, comforting me while taking her last journey home.
I Love You, Mom!

The Coming of the Hour

"And Isa (Jesus) will be a sign of the coming of the hour (of Judgement)."

This will be a clear global sign and he will communicate the truth about himself from the lies told concerning him and his mother. Many of you will be shocked and grieved after hearing his truth. Grieved because you followed and believed in the man-made lies invented by your own fellowship.

This event has not come to pass as yet so have patience with Mankind's evil ways, Allah (the Most High) is in complete control of His plan for Mankind.

The similitude of Isa (Jesus) is like that of Adam, Allah said "Be" and he was... The Creative Power of Allah is manifested in just a word or a thought. He does not require physical interaction with created Beings in order to create...

The Creator will return His appointed Prophet back to the Earth and there will be no more doubts, just the Sorting Out will remain as an event proclaimed...

The Righteous Shall Have No Fear On This Day...

The Fix Is In

The Fix Is In
Not by men of sin
Not by greed
or the will to win
A playing field to choose
Are the ground rules
A reward predetermined
One for showing gratitude
The other for being
boldly proud and selfishly rude
Eternal Life of Happiness
Eternal Life of Pain
Already Predetermined
Allow the proud to smile and grin
The last laugh washed free of sin
Remember the Fix Is already In
We the Righteous win in the end.
So it is written so His will be done!
Have Patience keep a steady pace
Already Predetermined for those who keep the faith.

Stay Focused

The Human Race created with a voice, created and given choice.
The Human Race given to choose between Righteousness or its many oppositions of which makes being righteous a wrong choice. Can you hear my voice?
The Seen and Unseen walk this Earth, Good and Evil taught from birth, the Righteous know that All Lives Matter but the infiltration of Evil cause some Lives to shatter...
Social Injustice seems to be a practice worldwide, overlooked by Evil Humans puffed up with powerful pride. Racial discrimination and Police brutality caused by the Evil infiltration of hate and stolen sovereignty.
Hate against one Race because of the Blackness of their skin, a worldwide hate for centuries, Stay Focused my friend... Paid infiltration to distract the topic at hand, Black people being murdered worldwide by a powerful Supremacy plan.
Yes, we know All Lives Matter, but Stay Focused my friend. Black People are being murdered worldwide by an Evil genocide. Stop trying to change the title, Black Lives is not All Lives Matter's rival!

Wake Up Righteous People! Humanity needs you, Slavery never ended 13 made it seem true, tricked you with word play and the law now cages you, free labor by privatized prisons as Master re-enslaves you.
Justice for All, fight oppression until it bleeds through…
The Revolution worldwide televised, the movement has splattered, Stay Focused before this Earth Shatters and yes, "Black Lives Matter!"
Whose side do you think God is on?
The Historical Answers can be found. The Righteous Win in the end.

Things Over Souls

It's amazing how you place value of things over souls.
You run to practice violence to protect a woven flag, a statue of pride you protect with AK held high acting mad.
A soul being choked while you stand on the sidelines.
Idolatry you protect, the living soul you forget all due to selfish pride.
We don't need another monument, we need laws of racial equality to federally circumvent…

North Philly Chapter 1

As I stepped out the front door once more from seeming rich the view was now poor.
Young eyes piercing the dawn lit sky as all life awakens from dreams and journeys that only God's Grace allows.
Day after day repetitively a practice, front door opens all seems to be in place, cobblestone echoes sounds of horseshoes clapping as birds sing the rhythms with wings flapping and changing pace.
Business is thriving, grocery corner stacked, barbershop full, lines for afro trimming and facial mud packs. Everyone says good morning and how do you do? Respect came natural not just for a few.
Awakened the next morning my dreams so confused, opened the front door to a horrible view. Dirt filled lots where groceries once plentiful, shattered green glass of a Thunderbird brew filled the dirt lots like seeds in soil.
From doors unlocked to now peepholes, triple deadbolt locked security doors are my first actions at dawn before opening the door with a Malcolm X visual plan, automatic weapon in hand for protection from my own clan.

Two enemies now, the government's systemic plan to destroy and dismantle a color brand, the other my own lost brother man.

My brother man who sells a corrupt brand to his neighborhood friends as the community walls crumble and they stumble back to dream of better days…

The respected hand that used to wave and speak now filled with drug swollen veins, dirty swollen toes and feet, what a sign of defeat.

Sucking a glass pipe as they plot to steal to meet their habitual needs as their dope fiend lean never seems to sleep.

Young and poor but never knew it until the community's walls began to fall from just a bite of forbidden fruit…

Your chapter one may differ from mine due to age and time, praying that yours was a pleasurable dream and not a horrible nightmare at all…

Message From the Author: The Truth Hurts

The Truth hurts those who faithfully follow and believe what they thought was truth but was mixed with falsehood. I already know that I will be hated and shunned by some for the truth that I am about to deliver but Allah (the Most High) states that it is really Him that they will hate since the truth comes from Him.

The Lies: Created things are Gods, Men are Gods, Statues are Gods, God is a trinity all three being one in the same.

The Truth: There is only One God (Allah, the Most High) known by 99 beautiful names that He is called. Early scriptures confirmed this fact and again confirmed in His last delivered Revelation.

The Lies: Mariam (Mary) the mother of Isa (Jesus) committed fornication and delivered a Bastard child. You can pray to Mary for forgiveness and assistance. Your prayers will be answered by worshipping statues of Mary.

The Truth: Mariam (Mary) was chosen by Allah to be the mother of His Chosen Prophet Isa (Jesus) he was born of miraculous birth with the power of just a breath and a word pronounced by The Creator, "Be." No man had ever touched her. She was a virgin when she gave birth to Isa. They both will be honored in this world and in the Hereafter.

The Lies: Isa (Jesus) is God, Isa is the son of God, Isa is within a Trinity - father, son and Holy Spirit all being one in the same. Isa created things, healed people and brought the dead back to life. Isa died on the cross for all man's sins. Isa rose from the dead. Accepting Isa as your lord and savior is the only way to get to Heaven.

The Truth: Allah Created Isa and instilled in him something of His Spirit and gave him a miraculous birth. Allah prepared the believers for Isa's coming in advance as a sign for them to know. When the miracles were seen by the believers Isa informed them that they were done by God's leave not by him. Isa is the son of Mariam, a miraculous created Being similar to Adam but not the son of God. One who is created cannot be God! Allah the Creator of all things, Isa a created man of miraculous birth and the Holy Spirit (the Angel Jibril or Gabriel) are not one in the same in a Trinity as Catholicism would have you believe. This article of faith in Catholicism is a man-made belief system and is not consistent with the long history of previously written Scripture or Revelations and the last written Revelation confirms this invention to be false. Isa was not tortured nor did he die on a cross but it was made to appear that way as an illusion. Since there was no death of Isa then the story of him rising from death is a lie.

If Isa was already prepared for his mission to die for all man's sins as Catholicism would have you to believe, he would have had no fear, he would not have to be hunted and sought after, he would have willingly given himself up for this his mission to save us all, but the collection of written Scriptures in the Bible don't communicate this fearless Jesus who is out to complete his mission to die for all man's sins… The scriptures have him hiding and denying who he is…

We do not require an intercessor for repentance. We can ask Allah to forgive us by speaking to Him directly at any time. Although you cannot see Him your Faith will assure you of His presence.

The Comforter

The Comforter
The Prophet Muhammad, Peace Be Upon him,
proclaimed the truth about Christ Jesus (Isa) the son of
Mary (Mariam).
The Holy Spirit Gabriel (the Angel Jibril) Testified
about Christ Jesus to the Comforter who then
communicated this testimony for all the world to know
and study.
The message has been with us since the late 700
hundreds A.D.
It confirms to those who follow the Jewish scriptures
that, Yes, Christ Jesus is the Prophet sent by Allah that
you were waiting for, he is not a blasphemer.
It also confirms to those who follow the Gospel that,
No, Christ Jesus was not God, nor the son of God and
the Trinity is something that man made up as a
falsehood. But Christ Jesus is Allah's Prophet and
Messenger.
There is only One God (Allah), the Creator of all
Things not to be joined with anyone or anything…
Reminder:
You shall not bow down to them or worship them; for
I, the LORD your God, am a jealous God…

Those of you still waiting for the Comforter and the Testimony of the Holy Spirit, the Holy Qur'an is your pathway to your quest...

The Comforter of which is the last Prophet who by divine inspiration delivered to the world Allah's last Revelation the seal of all the books that begin with the seven Holy verses has in fact already completed his mission.

Christ Jesus left you the key in his message, the Testimony has been delivered, the Comforter has spoken and the Truth is now known.

Seek and you shall find...

Study to show yourself approved!

The Holy Qur'an is the way and the Light.

God Hates Oppressors!

Our Creator stated for us to fight against Tyranny and Oppression! For it is better to die fighting against Tyranny and Oppression than to live under the rule of a Tyrant or an Oppressor!

The Creator gives us by example rules of engagement as it relates to war or fighting against a Tyrant or an Oppressor. We do not kill women or children, we don't lose focus by chasing material goods during the battle and if our Tyrant or Oppressor surrenders and harms you no more then allow them to leave or live in peace with them.

If your Tyrant or Oppressors break the treaty and still want for war or still kill you then slay them wherever you find them! Our Creator hates oppression and tyranny...

War is ugly but at times needed!

The Final Warning!

To my Jewish Brothers and Sisters
I Love those who profess their love for our Unseen Creator and the proof is seen in their righteous conduct.

To my Christian Brothers and Sisters I Love those who profess their love for our Unseen Creator and the proof is seen in their righteous conduct.

To my Muslim Brothers and Sisters
I Love those who profess their love for our Unseen Creator and the proof is seen in their righteous conduct.

Because of this love I have for the true family who reflect the signs of a good tree by the fruit that they produce and show their remembrance of our Unseen Creator I must remind you of the Final Warning:

After clear signs of His Unseen presence you shaped an image of a Golden Calf and worshipped it…

After warnings not to join anyone or anything with our Unseen Creator you worshipped Him in a Trinity…

You worship in the practice of Idolatry, shaping statues as gods, saints and intercessors to communicate through…

You even profess that He has begotten a son and worshipped the son of Mary as god, Oh! How small is your comprehension of our Unseen Creator…

Satan has accomplished in his time of respite to lead you in worshipping, praising and giving gratitude to others over the One and Only God who created everything in the universe of which praising Him only is due.
Those without faith can't believe in the Unseen so they choose to worship things they can see other than our Unseen Creator and this is a great sin punishable by a repeated death in the eternal Hell Fire…

Unless you Repent now, pray for forgiveness and amend your conduct for He forgives again and again because He is the only true Love you will ever have both now and in the Hereafter…
Peace Until Souls Meet Twice…

Once Clear Now Murky

From the beginning One God lessons taught! Successions of Prophets repeating this exact fact! So destroy your man made statuses no intercession required, pray directly to the Most High, He hears your call. Desist your false claims of partnership to His throne, no son does He claim and the Holy Spirit descends with the message for mankind by His command. The prophet line is promised through the seed of Abraham of which Paul was not, so revelations in the New Testament are false and made up! Check this if you will for truth will show that Christianity is not scared and hiding in caves no more. Christianity is the claim of the Powerful Governments of the world, so the second coming of Christ just who do you think He is really coming for? The Most High doesn't assist the haughty but more so the oppressed and the poor, check your history and stop being led from the Greatest of All!
Love and Righteousness is His call!

Like A Woman

Cleansing your hands right to left three times each,
while enunciating His Greatness,
a woman,
Cleansing your arms to elbows, what was said first
please repeat (three times each)
while enunciating His Greatness,
a woman,
Rinsing your mouth, nostrils, face and ears three times
each as woman falls gently passing through the
passages with strands or simply your smooth mountain
top creating streams, all while enunciating His
Greatness,
a woman,
Cleansing your feet right to left three times each, while
enunciating His Greatness,
a woman,
This Woman has you feeling refreshed, awake, alive,
vibrant, aware and ready!
Like a woman, the Creator supplies waters needed to
reproduce, purify and rid itself of properties no longer
required,
Water flows like the gentle touch of a woman's hand
passing over your body preparing you to embrace the
ultimate fulfillment of pleasure,
a woman,

This Woman (Water) prepared you mentally, physically and spiritually to stand before Him "the All Powerful" whom none other deserves to be Praised! Cleanliness is the next best thing to Godliness!

Not Even a Cure

Not even a guaranteed cure
Side effects galore body sore
Creating an internal war
False sense feeling secure
No, not trusting the treatment plan
Experts speaking false claims to man
Ultimatums pushed income hooked
No participation income took
Evil planned, created not pure
Giving ultimatums and not even a cure!
"Wear your mask until evil has passed!"
Hell is hot, prepared for all inhuman plots…
Governments twisting, turning, tightening their knots
Mandates for Not Even a Cure! How much more can we endure?

The Soul

The limitation of the shell
A temporary home not Heaven or Hell
Spirit expels, body simply a shell
Breath of life ignites the soul
The shell softens with motion of life
Spirit so powerful the body has might
The shell, the body without the soul
Just a fossil awaiting its fate?
The fate of judgment after a resurrection date…

The Righteous Shall Not Fear!
Peace Until…

My baba (father) El Hajj Nassardin Armin Abdullah
Retired barber, public school teacher and a legend of
his community
March 23, 1937 to September 9, 1999

My ummi (mom) Sayeeda Abdullah
Mother of six children and retired beautician
January 19, 1941 to December 26, 2019

My beautiful wife, Shanta' Tierra Williams

Wife Shanta' and her son, Kyree Nasir Williams

Gamel Adulce' Addin Ibn Abdullah

Husband and wife, June 18, 2014

Father, Nassardin, and son Gamel

Father, Gamel; son, Raheem; son, Kareem, and grandson Esaa

Youngest son, Tariq

My baba introduced me to Islam. We must keep the faith going…

The Holy Qur'an, Allah's gift to all mankind!

One of many Islamic mosques throughout the world

The Kabba In Mecca, Saudi Arabia

Allah (the Most High) Creator of all things hidden and seen…

I AM BLESSED AND INSPIRED!
KNOWLEDGE IS POWER WISDOM IS GAINED,
PASS IT ON…

 The
International
Library of Poetry

CERTIFICATE OF AUTHENTICITY

This certifies that the accompanied medallion is officially awarded by the *International Library of Poetry* in recognition of the recipient's poetic artistry, and it establishes them as an Editor's Choice Poet Scholar. The number below has been assigned, assuring its Limited Edition status.

ISSUE NUMBER: 1286

Gamel Adulce' Abdullah, author/poet

www.ingramcontent.com/pod-product-compliance
Lightning Source LLC
LaVergne TN
LVHW091559060526
838200LV00036B/918